CONTENTS

Introduction

How to set up the course

I have produced this manual in response to requests from hundreds of practitioners who have asked for a different approach to working with men who use violence against women.

I am Pat Craven a former probation officer who ran perpetrator programmes for Merseyside Probation Service between 1996 and 1998. I concluded that the programmes could have been much more successful if they were run in a very different style and by a different agency which was not subjected to the same constraints as a statutory body.

Imparting rules and instructions.
Everyone who attends is instructed to procure a copy of 'Living with the Dominator and 'How Hard Can It Be...?'. They must complete the written course before attending and bring their completed copy to the event.

The letter I send to trainees when the event is confirmed includes a timetable and a list of the rules. A template of the letter is available at the end of this manual. However at the beginning of the weekend I always restate the rules as I will describe in the instructions on how to facilitate session one.

The Gender of the Facilitators.
The facilitators can be men or women. They should be very familiar with the Freedom Programme and preferably have experience of facilitating it. They do not need to work with a man so he can be a 'role model.' Women only facilitators can give the message that women do not need a man to help them. However I have also trained several men who understand the programme and they are also eminently suitable.

Partners.

If a couple are still together, female partners should not be excluded. They should be in the room and be able to watch how he is reacting. They are the only people capable of assessing if he is learning anything or is changing. They are not only watching their own dominator but they are watching other men who are sitting in a group with him who are visibly changing. This is also has the additional advantage of bringing the men's shortened version of the Freedom Programme to women who may not otherwise have a chance to attend the women's programme.

Many other women who have already completed the women's programme then bring their abusers to the men's weekend as a condition of allowing him to stay in the relationship. Many men in this situation often agree to attend the weekend in the belief that they need not take it seriously and can get away with paying lip service to it.

Measuring outcomes.

Six out of 10 women who accompany their abusers tell me that the men have changed for the better. Four out of ten report no change but regard the event as a success because they can now make informed decisions.
Another way of evaluating success is to count what percentage of couples who attend have their children returned from the care of the local authority.

Duration

Unlike the women's programme the men's programmes should not be for a few hours a week. They are much more effective if compacted in to 2 days. This means they do not return to society in between sessions and have all their beliefs reinforced every time.

Reports

Facilitators should never write reports for courts or social care. They cannot assess if he has changed or not. They also have a vested interest in seeming to have succeeded and often get funding just because they say a man has changed. In other words women can be put at risk by facilitators who write such reports. The only person who can assess whether the man has genuinely changed is the partner who is watching him interact with other men
in his group.

Numbers

It is essential never to run the programme without sufficient men. It cannot work because success depends completely on the men learning from and informing each other. If there are not enough and the facilitator is actually telling the men what to think the programme will fail. They can only learn from each other. If the programme fails it will reinforce their behaviour instead of challenging it.

Facilitators need the flexibility to cancel a programme if too few turn up. I never confirm an event as viable until I have at least twenty five couples as I know from experience that only around half of them may turn up. The minimum number should be sixteen men plus their partners.

Always be prepared to cancel the weekend if too few attend and always make this clear to everyone who books a place.

Observers

I welcome observers but I insist that they join the groups. We are all anonymous and no group member must know the identity of another unless they are the partner who came with them.

Discipline

Trainees must behave or leave. Court mandates are self defeating. What is the point of a man attending because his solicitor can appeal against his removal? If he gets away with abusive behaviour it will reinforce his belief that abusive behaviour is acceptable because it has worked again.

It is crucial that when I facilitate this programme I have freedom to set my rules and to enforce them.
I will not change my rules to attract funding or meet guidelines set by other agencies.

No personal information

Dont let the men talk about themselves. They all sincerely believe that their victims force them to use violence. The men who come to my programmes arrive expecting me to help them cope with this horrible woman who forces them to assault her. If we allow them to air their very distorted views we are colluding with them and putting women in danger.

Enforcement

If anyone does not keep my rules I ask them to leave. If they refuse to go I will not continue and I close down the programme. I tell everyone to leave and ask those who really want to be there to leave their contact details with me so I can invite them when I arrange another date.

Usually when the miscreant has left everyone else remains and we continue with the programme. When I expel anyone it usually results in excellent cooperation from everyone else.

Safety

Some accuse the Freedom Programme for Men of endangering women. They imagine a situation where a man can become so enraged by the programme or indeed by being ejected from the group that they attack their partner in revenge. This betrays a lack of understanding of the way abusers behave.

When an abusive man commits an act of violence it is always planned. So in this situation he may have decided to be ejected from the course so he can blame her for insisiting that he attends. They do not just 'lose it' and attack their partners.

5

freedomprogramme@btinternet.com   www.freedomprogramme.co.uk

Timetable

Day 1

9.15 am	Arrival and coffee
9.30 am	Introduction to the Freedom Programme
11.00 am	Coffee break
11.15 am	The Bully
1.00 pm	Lunch
1.45 pm	Aspects of the Dominator. The Persuader, Headworker, Badfather, King of the Castle and Jailer
3.00 pm	Tea
3.15 pm	Aspects of the Dominator continued
5.00 pm	Finish

Day 2

9.30 am	The Sexual Controller
11.00 am	Coffee break
11.15 am	The Effects of Abuse on Children
1.00 pm	Lunch
1.45 pm	The Liar
3.00 pm	Tea
3.15 pm	The Liar continued
4.30 pm	Finish

freedomprogramme@btinternet.com   www.freedomprogramme.co.uk

Instruction manual.

Session 1. Introducing the Dominator (Living with the Dominator. Chapter 2, Pages 9 - 16) 9.30 - 11.00.

1.1 Introductions and 'ice breaker'

Welcome both men and women warmly. If we have at least sixteen men you can reassure everyone that the course can go ahead. Ensure that everyone has brought their own copy of 'Living with the Dominator' and 'How Hard Can it Be...?' If there are not enough men we all go home and try again in the future.

Separate the men and women. Then divide men and women in to their separate groups by giving each person in the room the name of the group they will join. For the first session you can use flower names. For example depending upon how many attenders there are choose Daffodils, Tulips, Snowdrops, Crocuses and Anemones. Try to aim for around five in a group.

Give everyone a name then direct all the Daffodils to one group of chairs, Tulips to another and so on. The men and women must go in to separate groups. For example women can be Daffodils and Tulips and men can be Snowdrops, Crocuses and Anemones. A list of suggestions for these names is included in the appendix.

Before we go any further remind every one of the rules. Unlike the women's programme, do not invite the men to suggest their own rules. Tell them exactly what the rules are.

1.2 The Rules

Turn off all mobile phones
There are no exceptions and it is not permitted to leave them on silent. If anyone cannot do this they must leave and arrange to attend next time.

One person - One voice
The Freedom Programme is a group work programme. We work together in small groups. This enables us to learn from each other by sharing our knowledge and experience. To function as a group we need to speak one at a time and listen to each other.

This means everyone must look at the speaker and not stare at the floor or their book or have private conversations.

Agree to differ
During the programme we all discuss a series of questions but there are no absolute answers. The aim of the programme is to help us to think about and question our society and ourselves.
No one has to have the last word.

No personal information
No one is to disclose any personal information.
This rule applies not only when we are working in the groups but also when we break for lunch or refreshments. If anyone breaks this rule I will eject them. I have spies in the groups who will tell me if anyone breaks this rule.

Pleasant and cooperative behaviour
If anyone uses any of the tactics of the dominator towards me or any other trainee I will ask the rest of the group to identify and name the tactic.

Child protection
If I learn that a child is in danger I have a statuary duty to inform the relevant authorities.

Join in
No sitting in silence. Everyone has to join in all discussions and contribute to the groups. We do not accept any man who does not join in and I will ask them to leave. This does not apply to the women who may have good reasons for reticence!

freedomprogramme@btinternet.com   www.freedomprogramme.co.uk

Introductions

In small groups, members must now introduce themselves to their companions in their small group in our 'Freedom Programme' way. Ask them to: 'Think of your first name, then think of a really pleasant non abusive description of yourself which begins with the same initial as your name.' Then think of a place where we may come from which also begins with the same letter. For example I am 'Perfect Pat' and I come from Paradise. If anyone cannot think of these names the other group members group can help them out if they just say their names. Everyone must do this to prove that they can behave in a pleasant and cooperative manner. Explain this to everyone before they all start to introduce themselves.

1.3 History

Read a synopsis of the history from the book 'Living with the Dominator'. This is found on pages 5 – 7.

1.4 Statistics Quiz

Read out each questions to all the groups. When you have read out a question invite everyone to discuss it and to come to a consensus. Give each group in turn a chance to answer first.

9

Statistics Quiz.

The facilitator asks the groups to discuss these statistics
in the form of a quiz.

The Quiz

1.   Domestic violence accounts for:

2% ☐   10% ☐   25% ☐   all reported violent crime.

2.   In Britain, a woman is killed by a violent partner
      or former partner every:

3 days ☐   week ☐   2 weeks ☐

3.   It is estimated that:

3% ☐   13% ☐   33% ☐

of all women experience domestic violence in their lifetime.

4.   How many times, on average, is a woman assaulted
      before she seeks help?

5 ☐   15 ☐   35 ☐

5.   On average, how many men a year are killed by their female partners
      or former partners?

22 ☐   52 ☐   112 ☐

6. On average, how many women a year are killed by their male partners or former partners?

12 ☐   52 ☐   112 ☐

7. How many women's refuges are there in England?

275 ☐   1000 ☐   5000 ☐

8. Is a woman:

less likely ☐   just as likely ☐   more likely ☐

to be assaulted when she is pregnant?

9. Domestic violence happens because of:

drink ☐   drugs ☐   stress ☐   mental illness ☐

unemployment ☐   none of these ☐

10. In Britain, police receive a complaint about domestic violence every.

60 seconds ☐   6 minutes ☐   6 hours ☐

11. In Britain, a woman is assaulted in her home every.

6 seconds ☐   60 seconds ☐   6 minutes ☐

THE ANSWERS

1. 25% of all reported crime (Amnesty UK, 2006)

2. Every 3 days (Home Office, 2007)

3. 33% (Home Office 2007). My experience with the Freedom Programme leads me to believe it is higher. Many of us do not realise we are being abused.

4. 35 (Amnesty UK, 2006)

5. 22 (Home Office, 2007)

6. 112 (Home Office, 2007)

7. 275 (Women's Aid, 2004) and, approximately, 1500 animal refuges

8. 3 times more likely to be injured when pregnant
    (Refuge, 2007)

9. None of these

10. 60 seconds   (Day to count, Elizabeth E. Stanko, 2000)

11. 6 seconds   (Day to count, Elizabeth E. Stanko, 2000)

12

     freedomprogramme@btinternet.com   www.freedomprogramme.co.uk

The Dominator and Mr Right.

Introduce the Dominator

Tell the group that they can see from the statistics that most abusers are men and that they use abusive behaviour to keep us women under control. Now they must open their books at the picture of the Dominator on page 11. Talk the groups through each type of abuse. You can then add more examples of each type of abuse for each group. If there is time, each group can invite one member to write down these examples. Then, ask the groups to share the new examples with the other groups.

Introduce Mr Right

Turn to page 14 and read out the last paragraph, which introduces Mr Right on page 15. Read all the examples of non-abusive behaviour.
Remind participants that the purpose of the Mr. Right handout is to reinforce the message that the behavior of the Dominator is abusive and not 'normal'. We will return to study him in greater detail later in the course.

Introduce the concept of beliefs

In the next part of the session, assist the group members to begin to understand why abusive men want to control women. To achieve this, explain the difference between thoughts and beliefs. Then explain to the group members that everyone behaves the way they do because of what they believe, not because of what they think. The group is invited to suggest what they think may be the difference between a thought and a belief. Then explain that our beliefs are the engines that drive our behavior. When we start to get to know our beliefs we start to understand ourselves.

We often do not see our beliefs as beliefs. We may see them as facts.

13

        freedomprogramme@btinternet.com   www.freedomprogramme.co.uk

Beliefs awareness exercise

Ask all men and women to stand and form a circle. Invite group members to step into the centre of the circle if they hold the sentiments expressed in this exercise. Remember to ask them to step back out again after each question.

Do I believe it is important to keep the air we breathe clean?
Do I drive a car?
If the answer to both questions is yes, what do I really believe about my needs and the needs of the planet?

Do I disapprove of bullying?
Have I ever shouted at my children, partner or the dog?
If the answer to both questions is yes, what do I really believe about bullying?
If group members respond to both (and most will) they will also recognise that they believe that bullying works and it is acceptable if you have a good excuse.
I give the example of shouting at the dog who has messed on the carpet. Beliefs are: I own the dog. I am superior. The dog is inferior. Bullying works. Bullying is fine if you can justify it. Remind everyone that the Bully also holds these beliefs.

Do I believe in keeping my body healthy?
Do I smoke, drink or eat too much?
If the answer to both questions is yes, what do I really believe?
Most of the group will respond to this and then I usually use my former addiction to cigarettes to illustrate these beliefs. Together, we will agree that when I smoked I believed that although cigarettes did kill other people, I did not believe they would kill me. This example of holding two conflicting or irrational beliefs can be compared to the dissonant beliefs of abusive men. This is 'cognitive dissonance.'

Do I believe women have a right to say no to sex?
Tell everyone to step in if they agree with this statement.

Have I ever huffed and puffed and sulked?
Only the men should step in for this part of the question.
Point out that, if this last example is used, men may well believe that women do not have the right to say no to sex. We will return to this theme later in the programme.

14

     freedomprogramme@btinternet.com   www.freedomprogramme.co.uk

The beliefs of the Dominator

At this point, group members are invited to consider which beliefs abusive men hold. Go through the Dominator graphic. Ask the groups what each aspect of the Dominator believes.
e.g. 'What does the Bully believe about the use of violence and the status of women compared to men?' 'Where does the Jailer believe women should be?'

We will identify that the Dominator believes that it is OK to use violence if you have a good excuse and that it is acceptable to use such violence to control women. We will recognise that he believes women are inferior beings who need to be controlled.

Then ask the group where such beliefs come from.
They will suggest childhood and society and we will begin to discuss how they are reinforced by the society in which we live. Emphasise that the Dominator is not a deviant but is motivated by the beliefs of the society in which he lives.

Then lay the ground for the rest of the programme by explaining that most of the sessions will examine the tactics used by each aspect of the Dominator, the beliefs which motivate the tactics, and the origins and reinforcements of these beliefs.

Add that we will also end all sessions on a positive note, usually discussing the attributes of a non- abusive man.

1.7 Why Do Women Not Go Back to Abusive Men?
Staying in the large group, invite everyone to offer suggestions as to how a woman's life is improved when the Dominator is no longer in the home. What can we do now that we could not do before? Answer in the role of the woman. e.g. 'I can cuddle my children'.

16

 freedomprogramme@btinternet.com   www.freedomprogramme.co.uk

Session 2. The Bully (Living with the Dominator.
Chapter 3, Pages 17 - 25)

From now on, this is the format for each session.
Put everyone into small groups. Use different group names for each session to make sure that by the end of the course all the men and women have worked together in their separate groups. Ask everyone to introduce themselves to their new groups with the Freedom names.

This and all the rest of the sessions begin with a quiz about the Dominator. Read a tactic and ask the groups to call out which aspect of the dominator uses each tactic. Remind everyone that the aim of the quiz is not so much to get all the answers right, but more to help us to identify and name abusive behaviour when we see it.

The Quiz.

Tactic.

1. Sulks
2. Tells me my tits are too small
3. Goes out of the room when my friends visit
4. Says' 'It was only a push'
5. Tells the kids I am stupid
6. Expects his dinner to be ready whenever he walks through the door
7. Invites my friend to have a threesome
8. Tells me he will kill himself if I leave

Answers

1. The Bully
2. The Headworker
3. The Jailer
4. The Liar
5. The Badfather
6. The King of the Castle
7. The Sexual Controller
8. The Persuader

2.2 Question Sheets for the Bully

These sheets are also available to print out from this manual.
Invite the groups to allow one of their members to volunteer to make notes.
Emphasise that we want volunteers not conscripts. Tell them that we also need
one person in each group to read out questions from 'How Hard Can it Be?'
Everyone else now must close their books.
Tell the groups to answer one section at a time and not to move on until the
facilitator instructs them. Walk round and listen to make sure they all read out
each question.

Tell the group members to answer all the questions in role. In most of the of the
question sheets the first three questions of the abuser and the last should be
answered in the role of non abusive man.

e.g. A sample answer for the tactics of the Bully is 'I shout'.
e.g. A sample answer for the beliefs of the Bully could be 'Women need to be
kept in order'.
e.g. A sample answer for 'Where does the Bully get his beliefs could be 'Most
religions do not allow women to be priests' which gives a strong message that we
are not good enough.

This provides a safe space for anyone who wishes to talk about their own
situation. No one should ask anyone else: 'Are you in role?'

When answering the next question ask the groups to answer in role as a woman.
Please note that the question sheets for men do not include the question "Which
beliefs do women share?'
e.g. A sample answer to the questions
'How are women affected by being bullied' could be
'I am walking on eggshells and can never relax'

When you come to the last question which asks about the non abusive
counterpart to the dominator you instruct the groups to answer this in the role
of this non abusive man.
e.g. A sample answer to the question
'How does the friend behave?' could be
'I have a sense of humour and do not have to have the last word'.

The quiz and the completion of the questions sheet take one hour.
When all the small groups have answered all the questions then ask each writer
to read their answers to the larger groups. Make sure they do not repeat
anything which has already been said.
This should take 30 minutes.

Question Sheet for The Bully

The tactics of the Bully
Answer in role as the Bully.
Make a list of as many as you can think of. We are not asking for examples of violence. Concentrate on intimidation.
How does the Bully use his body language to intimidate?
How does he use every bit of his body?
Think of his fingers, toes and eyes.
Don't ask what he says, but how he says it?

What does the Bully believe?
Answer in role as the Bully.
What does he believe about violence, "real" men and the status of women compared to men? Does he believe women need controlling/protecting? What does he believe about men who do not bully?

Where do his beliefs come from and how are they reinforced?
Answer in role as the Bully
What about culture, sports and institutions such as the armed forces?
Only discuss your OWN culture. Consider religion, music and all forms of media including film. Give examples.

How are we affected by being bullied in this way?
Answer as a woman.
How do I feel all the time?
How may I behave?

How does the Friend behave and what does he believe?
Answer as the man who is a 'friend'.
Look at his body language.
What are his eyes like? What is his voice like?
What does he believe about women?
Does he like women?
What does he believe about the use of violence?

20

Notes for the facilitator when taking the feedback.

The beliefs of the Bully

One belief that is usually identified is that the Bully believes he is superior to women. When this is identified, it is helpful to create him as an imaginary Dominator. He can be christened Roger, for example. The facilitator places Roger in an empty chair and invites participants to ask him questions and provide the answers for him.

The dialogue will begin by asking him why he is superior to women in general and his partner in particular. It will end when it becomes clear that this belief is founded on physical strength and the facilitators ensure that the final part of the dialogue makes clear that greater physical strength is not an indicator of greater ability.

Example of dialogue with Roger

"Tell me Roger why do you feel you are superior to women?"
"Because I earn the money in this family"
"But Roger, your partner actually earns more than you"
"Possibly, but I am more intelligent and do a more important job."
"So what about your partner's degree in Rocket Science as opposed to your NVQ level 1 in Painting and Decorating".
"But all she does is sit around all day writing and talking. I do real work."
"What do you mean by real work Roger? Surely she has more effect on more people than you?"
"I mean man's work, physical work".
"So what is it about this that makes you superior Roger?"
"I am stronger than her, I can lift more than her, and I can do more than her".
"So you believe that all physically strong creatures are superior to all less strong creatures?"
"Of course"
"So, Roger, why isn't there an elephant in the White House and a gorilla running Microsoft?"

freedomprogramme@btinternet.com   www.freedomprogramme.co.uk

Explain that Roger is conflating two distinct and different concepts. Physical strength and superiority are not the same.

Finish the session by reminding the group that the contents of this session are covered in pages 17 – 25 of 'Living with the Dominator'.

1.45.p.m. Aspects of the Dominator. Badfather, Headworker, Jailor, Persuader, King of the Castle.

Mix up the groups again and tell them to introduce themselves to their new group using their Freedom Programme names.

Do 5 quizzes. Explain that we are going to have a taster of each aspect.

Explain that each group will a give a little presentation to rest of the trainees.

Limit the time spent on on each question to 5 minutes. Go round the groups to ensure that they keep up with the timing and read all the new questions out.

Start to take the feedback at 2.30.p.m. Try to complete the Badfather and Headworker before the break.

3.00.p.m. Tea.

3.15.p.m. Aspects of the Dominator continued. Save the Jailer until the last presentation at about 4.00.p.m.

Ask them to stand in a circle.
Finish off with the going to college role play on page 27 of the manual.

4.30.   FINISH

Session 3. The Badfather (Living with the Dominator. Chapter 4, Pages 27 – 34)

3.1 The Quiz

Tactics

1. Smashes things
2. Tells other people my secrets
3. Tells me my friend made a pass at him
4. Says I started it
5. Uses the courts to get access to the children
6. Nags until I agree to sex
7. Takes all the money
8. Says he has nowhere else to go

Answers

1. The Bully
2. The Headworker
3. The Jailer
4. The Liar
5. The Badfather
6. The Sexual Controller
7. The King of the Castle
8. The Persuader

23

     freedomprogramme@btinternet.com   www.freedomprogramme.co.uk

3.2 Question Sheet for The Badfather

Tactics of the Badfather
Answer in role as the Badfather.
How does the Badfather ensure that I cannot control the children?
How does he use the children to isolate me?
How does he use the children to persuade me to have him back after violence?
How does he use the children to intimidate me? He can do this when we are still together or when I have separated from him.
How will he use other agencies to use the children to abuse me?

His beliefs
Answer in role as the Badfather.
What does he believe about childcare and real men?
Does he believe that women can cope with children without a man, any man, in the house?
Who does he think has rights? Women, children, or him?
Does he believe violence affects children? Does he care?

Origins and reinforcements
Answer in role as the Badfather.
Where does he get his beliefs from?
Consider political propaganda.
Consider the messages he gets from the media about the need for a father figure.
What do the family courts tell him?
What message does he get from pressure groups?
What messages has he had from other agencies?

How are we affected?
Answer in role as a woman.
How am I affected when he uses access and the courts to harass me?
How am I affected when he uses the children to isolate me?
How am I affected when he turns the children against me?

The Goodfather
Role play the Goodfather.
How does the Goodfather behave towards me in front of the children?
How does he behave towards the children?
What does he believe about childcare?

Take the feedback then finish the session by reminding the group that the contents of this session are covered in pages 27 – 34 of 'Living with the Dominator'.

freedomprogramme@btinternet.com   www.freedomprogramme.co.uk

Session 4. The Headworker (Living with the Dominator. Chapter 6, Pages 47 – 56)

The Quiz

Tactic

1. Grits his teeth
2. Has affairs with other women
3. Has affairs with my friends
4. Tells me I made him abusive
5. Comes and goes as he pleases
6. Denies paternity
7. Cries on the doorstep
8. Ejaculates prematurely and blames me.

Answers

1. The Bully
2. The Headworker
3. The Jailer
4. The Liar
5. The King of the Castle
6. The Badfather
7. The Persuader
8. The Sexual Controller

26

freedomprogramme@btinternet.com   www.freedomprogramme.co.uk

Question sheet for the Headworker.

Tactics of the Headworker.
Answer as the Headworker.
How does the Headworker make me feel ugly, useless, stupid and mad?

What does the Headworker believe?
Answer as the Headworker.
What does he believe about our competence and intelligence?
What does he believe women are placed on this earth for?
What is our function?

Where do such beliefs come from and how are they reinforced?
Answer as the Headworker.
Consider language. What words are used about us to indicate that
we are stupid?
What words indicate that we are pieces of meat?
Think of the history of psychiatry.
Think of magazines. Think of music and insidious messages in advertising.
Think of a very famous radio presenter who consistently makes sexist jokes.
Think about the content of jokes about women.

Effects of those beliefs on behaviour
Answer as a woman.
How am I affected by living with a Headworker?
How am I affected by all his tactics?
How are all women affected by living in a society, which holds the beliefs of
the Headworker?

The Confidence Booster
Answer as the male opposite to the Headworker.
How does the Confidence Booster behave to me?
What does he believe about women?

Take the feedback and read out the Nelson Mandela story on page 55 of
'Living with the Dominator'. Remind everyone that the contents are covered
on pages 47 – 56.

Session 5. The King of the Castle (Living with the Dominator. Chapter 9, Pages 77 - 86)

5.1 The Quiz

Tactics

1. Kicks walls
2. Does not use my name
3. Does not take the key when he goes out
4. Says he suffers from Gulf War Syndrome
5. Contradicts my instructions to the children
6. Pretends he can't cook
7. Says: 'Unless you have me back, I will follow you to the ends of the earth!'
8. Tells me I am unnatural if I refuse sex

Answers

1. The Bully
2. The Headworker
3. The Jailer
4. The Liar
5. The Badfather
6. The King of the Castle
7. The Persuader
8. The Sexual Controller

freedomprogramme@btinternet.com   www.freedomprogramme.co.uk

Question sheet for the King of the Castle.

Tactics of the King of the Castle.
Answer as the King of the Castle.
How does he manipulate me so I will do all household tasks with out being aware of it?

How does he get me to do all the washing? How does he get me to do the cooking? How does he get me to do the cleaning? How does he make sure I know where things are and that I put things away? What is the question he will ask?
How does he get me to be in charge of menus? What question will he ask? How does he begin to control the money? How will he ensure he is in charge of the television?

The beliefs of the King of the Castle.
Answer as the King of the Castle.
What does he believe about the status of the occupation of housework?
What sort of people should therefore do his housework?
Would a "real man" pay someone to do his housework?
What does he believe about men who do their share of housework?

Where do these beliefs come from and how are they reinforced?
Answer as the King of the Castle.
Consider his childhood. Look at advertisements. Consider soap opera, films and books. What are women seen to be doing? Consider social policies and commonly used phrases which describe women?

How are we affected by the tactics used by the King of the Castle?
Answer as a woman.
How am I affected by being treated as a skivvy without rights or respect?
How are we all affected by the beliefs of the society in which we live?

How does the Partner behave?
Answer as the Partner.
He is the non-abusive counterpart to the King of the Castle. What does he do around the house and what does he believe?

Take the feedback and read 'The Good Wives Guide' from page 82.
Remind everyone that the contents of this session are covered on pages 77 – 86 of 'Living with the Dominator'.

Session 6. The Persuader Living with the Dominator.
Chapter 11, Pages 99 - 109)

The Quiz

Tactic

1. Drives too fast
2. Tells me I am useless
3. Moves me to a strange town
4. Attempts suicide
5. Says I made him abuse me
6. Says I am a bad mother
7. Refuses to have sex with me
8. Complains if I spend money on myself

Answers

1. The Bully
1. The Headworker
3. The Jailor
4. The Persuader
5. The Liar
6. The Badfather
7. The Sexual Controller
8. The King of the Castle

Question sheet for the Persuader

Tactics of the Persuader
Answer as the Persuader.
How does he make me feel sorry for him?
How does he indicate to me that he cannot cope without me?
Will he also use other people to influence me?
How will he use the children to persuade me to have him back?
What threats or promises may he make?
How will he make me jealous to persuade me to have him back?
How will he use the excuses of the Liar to increase his level of control?

Beliefs of the Persuader
Answer as the Persuader.
Who does he believe is responsible for his behaviour and his well-being?
Does he believe he has to pay any price for his violence and abuse? Does he believe his behaviour is in any way unacceptable? Who does he believe is allowed to end the relationship and whom does he believe is not?

Where do these beliefs come from and how are they reinforced?
Answer as the Persuader.
Consider popular music, country and western and blues.
Consider the law. Consider all the people he may go to for help. How might their responses reinforce his beliefs? For example, he may visit a bolloxologist for help to manage his 'anger'.

How am I affected by The Persuader?
Answer as a woman.
How am I affected by being made to feel sorry for him?
How am I affected by his threats?

The Negotiator
Answer as the Negotiator.
How does he behave if I want to end the relationship? Whose welfare will he consider? What does he believe?

Take the feedback and remind everyone that the contents of this session are covered on pages 99 - 109 of 'Living with the Dominator'.

31

Session 7. The Jailer. (Living with the Dominator. Chapter 7, Pages 57 – 63)

7.1 The Quiz

Tactic

1. Displays weapons
2. Makes me feel guilty
3. Tells me my friends don't like me
4. Says it only happened because he was drunk
5. Says I can leave but the children stay
6. Says he "helps me" with the housework
7. Threatens to kill the children if I leave
8. Bribes me to have sex by offering to buy me a new winter coat

Answers

1. The Bully
2. The Headworker
3. The Jailer
4. The Liar
5. The Badfather
6. The King of the Castle
7. The Persuader
8. The Sexual Controller

Question sheet for the Jailer.

Tactics used by the Jailer.
Answer as the Jailer.
How does the Jailor stop me seeing friends?
How does he stop me working?
How does he keep me in the house?
How does he cut me off from my family?

The Jailer's beliefs.
Answer as the Jailer.
Where does the Jailor believe women should be?
What would he believe about a man who did not keep his partner locked away?
What does he believe we will all do if we do go out?
What does he believe we all are?

Where do all these beliefs come from and how are they reinforced?
Answer as the Jailer.
Consider language and commonly used phrases.
Consider social traditions, sports and education.
Think about social policies and advertisements.
When did women get the vote?

How do our beliefs and experience affect our behaviour?
Answer as a woman.
How am I affected by being kept in the house?
How am I affected by being prevented from working?
How am I affected by being cut off from our friends and family?
How are we all affected by our widely shared beliefs?

The Liberator.
Answer as the male opposite to the Jailer.
How does the Liberator behave? Consider his reactions to my desire to work, get out of the house and meet my friends?
How does he behave to my friends and family?
What does he believe about me?
Does he trust his partner?

33

 freedomprogramme@btinternet.com   www.freedomprogramme.co.uk

Take the feedback and remind everyone that the contents are covered on pages 57 – 63 of 'Living with the Dominator'.

Add this to the feedback

The Jailer makes our family and friends unwelcome by watching sports or porn on TV at earsplitting volume. He will be wearing his boxer shorts (if we are lucky). He will be holding the remote in his right hand and fiddling with his nuts with the left. He may also be farting, burping, snorting or cutting his toenails. 'Whoops a toenail has just dropped in to my mother's tea!)

I am going to college

Ask everyone to stand in a circle.
Invite everyone to imagine that they are all my husbands. When we married, I left college to bring up the children on the condition that, when the children are old enough and if we have enough money I can go back.

The children are now old enough and we are rolling in money. I greet you all on your return from work armed with my prospectus.

All my husbands must now use the tactics of the Dominator which we have discussed today to persuade me not to go. When they have succeeded, I ask them to repeat the exercise and try to persuade me not to go to college WITHOUT using the tactics of the Dominator. If they do, I name the tactic, e.g. Liar or Headworker. The group soon realises that they cannot persuade me not to go to college without using abusive behaviour and therefore the very act of trying to do so is abusive.

Finally, we repeat the exercise, but this time they are the Liberators, Confidence Boosters, etc and I am going to college!

END OF DAY ONE.

DAY TWO

MIX UP THE GROUPS BEFORE EVERY SESSION.

Session 8.The Sexual Controller (Living with the Dominator.
Chapter 8, Pages 65 - 76) 9.30.a.m. to 11.00.a.m.

Tactic

1. Stalks me
2. Makes me think I am going mad by moving furniture and then denying it
3. Goes everywhere with me
4. Says he was abusive because he was jealous
5. Asks the children to check up on me
6. Says I must be a lesbian if I say no to sex
   (Bless him! He thinks it is an insult!)
7. Ignores the housework until I do it
8. Promises that he will see a relate counsellor if I have him back

Answers

1. The Bully
2. The Headworker
3. The Jailer
4. The Liar
5. The Badfather
6. The Sexual Controller
7. The King of the Castle
8. The Persuader

35

freedomprogramme@btinternet.com   www.freedomprogramme.co.uk

Question sheet for the Sexual Controller.

Note that there are 2 separate questions about his tactics. Allow at least 3 minutes for each one then revert to the usual format for the rest of the questions.

Tactics of the Sexual Controller
Answer as the Sexual Controller.
How does he make me have sex when I do not want it?
How does he use sex as a weapon to degrade and defeat me?

The beliefs of the Sexual Controller
Answer as the Sexual Controller
What does he believe about men and women?
What does he believe we are actually for?
Does he believe we have any other function apart from providing sex?
What does he believe about out rights and his rights?
Does he like women?

Where do these beliefs come from and how are they reinforced?
Answer as the Sexual Controller
Law. Media. Magazines. Newspapers. The medical profession.
Fine art. Religion. Music. History. Give examples.

Effects of the Sexual Controller on women.
Answer as a woman.
How am I affected by living with a sexual controller?
How are we all affected by living in a society which holds these beliefs?

The Lover

Answer as this a non abusive man.

How does he behave sexually?

Does he show me affection?

What does he believe about women?

Does he like us?

Would he go to a lap-dancing club?

If not, why not?

What does he believe about sex?

Please note that the facilitator does not give an opinion about the lap-dancing club.

Take the feedback and remind everyone that the contents are covered on pages 65 – 76 of 'Living with the Dominator'.

At the end of the feedback read out the 'Good Wives Guide to Sex' as a further example of how society has reinforced the beliefs of the Sexual Controller.

The Good Wives Guide to Sex

This an actual extract from a sex education book for girls printed in the early 60s in the UK and explains why the world was much happier and peaceful then...!

'When retiring to the bedroom prepare yourself for bed as promptly as possible. Whilst feminine hygiene is of the most upmost importance , your tired husband does not want to queue for the bathroom as he would have to do for his train.

But remember to look your best when going to bed. Try to achieve a look that is welcoming without being obvious. If you need to apply face cream or hair rollers wait until he is asleep as this can be shocking to a man last thing at night.

When it comes to the possibility of intimate relations with your husband it is important to remember your marriage vows and in particular your commitment to obey him.

37

If he feels that he need to sleep immediately then so be it. In all things be led by your husbands wishes: do not pressure him in any way to stimulate intimacy. Should your husband suggest congress then agree humbly all the while being mindful that a man's satisfaction is more important than that a woman's. When he reaches his moment of fulfilment a small moan from yourself is encouraging to him and quite sufficient to indicate any enjoyment that you may have had.

Should your husband suggest any of the more unusual practices be obedient and uncomplaining but register any reluctance by remaining silent. It is likely that your husband will then fall promptly asleep so adjust your clothing, freshen up and apply your night time face and hair care products.

You may then set the alarm so that you can arise shortly before him in the morning. This will enable you to have his morning cup of tea ready when he awakes.'

The Effects of Domestic Abuse on Children
(Living with the Dominator. Chapter 5, Pages 35 – 46)
11.30.a.m. to 1.00.p.m.

The Quiz

Tactic

1. Sulks
2. Tells me I am ugly
3. Causes a row when I want to go out
4. Denies he was abusive when challenged
5. Refuses to 'baby-sit'
6. Burns the breakfast
7. Threatens to report me to Social Services if I leave him
8. Rapes me when I am asleep

Answers

1. The Bully
2. The Headworker
3. The Jailer
4. The Liar
5. The Badfather
6. The King of the Castle
7. The Persuader
8. The Sexual Controller

freedomprogramme@btinternet.com   www.freedomprogramme.co.uk

Question Sheet for Session the Effects on Children.

What do children need?
Answer in the role of the pregnant mother.
The first group to consider is the pregnant mother, an unborn child and a newborn baby. What do they need? You may like to consider the needs of the mother first and then see that the other needs flow from them.
e.g. 'I need good food so my unborn child can develop properly.'

Answer as the parent.
The next category deals with the needs of a six-year-old. Please list everything that you can think of that a six-year-old needs to develop successfully. Be specific. Don't just say things like 'care.' Define exactly what this means.
e.g. 'My six year old needs a lot of sleep.'

Answer as the teenager.
What does a teenager need? Consider whether the needs of the previous categories are linked to the needs of the teenager.
e.g. 'I still need cuddles.'

Effects of domestic abuse on children

Answer in the role of the mother again.
What happens to this group when there is a violent abusive man in the house? Consider how the mother is affected and then discuss how this affects the unborn child and the new baby. Do not assume that women in this situation are poor, unemployed stupid, drug addicts or drunks.
Answer in the role of the mother again.
e.g. 'My baby died after he kicked me in the stomach.'

Answer as the mother.
Now consider the six-year-old. Consider that our child is now six years older. Remember all the effects on the first group. Now consider the situation six years later. See how much worse things are. Consider the beliefs our six-year-old will be developing.
e.g 'My child wets the bed."My child has tantrums to get their own way.'

40

freedomprogramme@btinternet.com   www.freedomprogramme.co.uk

Answer as the teenager.
Finally, now have a look at the teenager. All the effects on the baby and the six-year-old have now accumulated in the teenager. How are they affected and what will they now believe?
e.g 'I have run away from home.'

Home improvements

Answer as the mother.
Now list how the lives of an unborn child, pregnant women newborn child are improved without the Dominator. Imagine he has left or stopped being abusive when I am six months pregnant. I will then have the last three months without abuse. How will everything have improved for my new baby and me? Don't forget that I am attending the Freedom Programme and am receiving support and making friends.
e.g. 'My baby was born alive'.

Answer as the mother.
Now list the improvements for a six-year-old. He has left or changed when our child is five. We have been free of abuse for a year.
e.g. 'My child had a birthday party.' 'The house is always full of their friends.'

Answer as the teenager.
Now list the improvements for a fifteen-year-old. He has left or changed when our child is thirteen. We have been free of abuse for two years.
e.g 'I can cuddle my mother.'

Take the feedback then finish the session by reminding the group that the contents of this session are covered in pages 35 – 46 of 'Living with the Dominator'.

The Liar (Living with the Dominator. Chapter 10, Pages 87 - 97)
1.45.p.m to 4.00.p.m.

The Quiz

Tactic

1. Swings his foot
2. Hides my shoes
3. Tells me I must be suffering from PMT
4. Says I must have him back because he has cancer
5. Says any red-blooded man would kill his wife if he found her in bed with another man
6. Hits me when the children are in the house
7. Has his own chair that no one else is allowed to use
8. Asks the surgeon to stitch me up tight after childbirth

Answers

1. The Bully
2. The Jailer
3. The Headworker
4. The Persuader
5. The Liar
6. The Badfather
7. The King of the Castle
8. The Sexual Controller

freedomprogramme@btinternet.com   www.freedomprogramme.co.uk

The Liar and 'Rules of the Game' (Living with the Dominator.
Chapter 10. Page 87 - 98)

Open the book at page 88 and look at 'Rules of the Game'.
Explain the graphic. Talk them through all the boxes. Then ask members of each
group to explain what they have just heard to other group members.

What are the Rules?
Answer as the man.
Write a a list of eight Rules of the Game. Use phrases like: "Women should..."
"She should always..." "She should never..." I should be able to..."

Abusive Tactics
Have a look at the Dominator on page 11 and note an example of which aspect of
the Dominator keeps which rule in place. For example, "She should never answer
back" would be kept in place by the Bully. You can note the answers at the side of
your rules above. Initials such as KOC (King of the Castle) will suffice.

Breaking the Rules

Answer as the woman.
How do I break the rules? Don't forget that I often do not know what the rules
are. One of the rules is that I should always know what the rules are. When
considering how I break the rules, look at the list you have written. I could break
each rule in many different ways, either accidentally or deliberately. This time
write these examples in my voice, for example. I let the midwife into the house'
or 'I left him.'

Excuses for Violence (Winding himself up)

Answer as the man.
Remember he is giving himself these excuses before using violence to justify
what he has already decided to do.
Write his excuses in his voice. Use emotive language and remember that he has
not yet hit me. Do not spare the bad language. It will be easier for him to hit me
if he convinces himself that I am not human.

43

     freedomprogramme@btinternet.com   www.freedomprogramme.co.uk

Trying to put the rules back in place by using the tactics of the Liar Answer as the man.

How does he now get the rules back in place using Minimisation, Denial and Blame?

Give examples of the "only" word to make the abuse seem less than it was.

What will he say to deny that anything happened?

What will he blame? Make a list including as many medical conditions as possible. Don't forget that he will rarely give the real reason, which is that I broke the rules. He will, however, blame me. What will he say?

How are women affected by the behaviour of the Liar?

Answer as a woman.

Make a list of as may ways as you can think of which may describe how I am affected by these complicated tactics.

Feedback

Seat the group in a large circle. Tell everyone to sit beside members of their group in the large circle. Include men and women.

First tell everyone that they will now read back the "Rules" in role. To get into the part, we all need to sit like the Dominator. Demonstrate the crotch thrust.

Then say 'Hands on nuts!' (Remembering the Jailer).

Now, ask someone from each group to read one rule at a time. Remind everyone that the Dominator believes these rules are natural and normal so his tone can reflect this by being reasonable and relaxed.

Go round the circle as fast as you can and feel the atmosphere build up.

We do not ask the groups to read out which aspect of the Dominator keeps each rule in place. That was a useful revision exercise, which also increases our understanding of the whole process of power and control. We now go back to using women's voices and read out one example of how we broke a rule. Again, go round the circle fast and feel the atmosphere build up.

Now we have listed how we break the rules, we need to go back to the voice of the Liar and "wind him up." This time they can use very emotive tones to reflect the fact that the Liar is 'winding himself up'.

44

freedomprogramme@btinternet.com   www.freedomprogramme.co.uk

When you have read all the 'wind ups' out, you can do the role play.

Role Play
Leave the large circle. Everyone stand in two rows which face each other forming a corridor between them.

The facilitator invites one of the men to play her husband. They stand together at one end of the corridor. The facilitator says to the group, 'This my husband. Please tell the group your name?'

He introduces himself and then the facilitator tells the group this history. He may choose to call himself George.

She continues:
' George and I have been married for many years and he has been continually violent and abusive. Recently a neighbour called the police and he was convicted of assault and ordered to complete a perpetrator programme. Well he has been attending regularly and has not been violent again.
However, I have also been going to the Freedom Programme and I have realised that he is still using all the other controlling tactics of the Dominator.
So today I decided to set a test to see if he has changed at all. I went off to Tescos and took my time. I even met one of my Freedom Programme friends for coffee.
When I got back he was winding himself up and shouting accusations at me. This time I stood up to him and told him that it was obvious that he had not changed at all. I told him to get out.

He argues and bullies but eventually does leave saying he is going out to cool off. He then walks up and down between the rows of chairs listening to the others all shouting out the thoughts that he is using to 'wind himself up'.

Explain to the group and to your 'husband' that you will all enact this now. Pick up a bag and call out 'Hi George. I am back from Tesco's!' Enact the scene as instructed and when he comes back down the row to 'hit you' take him by the hand. Turn him to face the group and ask for a round of applause for his performance and then ask for another for yours.

Ask him how he now feels and if he would have come back to hit us.
Set everyone back in the large circle and take the feedback on the minimisation, denial and blame in the voice of the Dominator.

Then feedback the effects on the woman.
Follow that with the effects on us and finish with our honest
and accountable man.

The Truthteller

Ask the big group

'Which part of the cycle of "Rules of the Game" does he have to change to
change his behaviour?

Is he actually angry or is all this manufactured outrage?

Remind everyone that the contents of this session are covered on pages 87 –
97 of 'Living with the Dominator'.

 freedomprogramme@btinternet.com   www.freedomprogramme.co.uk

The Final Quiz

Tactics

1. Cracks knuckles.
2. Takes the buggy in the boot of the car
3. Uses the word "woman" as an insult
4. Promises to go to anger management (bolloxology)
5. Makes jokes about me to the children
6. Asks,:"Where is my clean shirt?"
7. Visits a lap dancing club
8. Says he was abusive because he is insecure

Answers

1. The Bully
2. The Jailer
3. The Headworker
4. The Persuader
5. The Badfather
6. The King of the Castle
7. The Sexual Controller
8. The Liar

FINISH

Letter of instruction.

Dear Couple.
In theory we now have enough people to go ahead with our healthy relationship weekend on ....

Please come to ..... and carefully follow these instructions.

If a man is in a relationship I will not accept him on to the course unless he attends with his partner. She must also read the book 'Living With the Dominator' and bring it with a completed copy of the 'Home Study Course for Women' with her to the event. This means that everyone who attends must bring both books to use within the course. The online programme will not suffice.

These strict rules apply
Sometimes even though enough people have booked places occasionally they do not all attend. I will not go ahead on the day if I do not have enough. Please make sure you understand this as some of you travel from abroad.
No one is allowed to discuss any personal information during the course.
All mobile phones must be switched off.
Anyone who does not behave in a pleasant, good humored and cooperative manner will be instructed to leave.
I do not issue certificates and never write reports for courts or any other agencies.

Suggested names

Daffodil	Tulip	Snowdrop	Hyacinth	Crocus
Maserati	Alfa Romeo	Ferrari	Rolls	Bentley
Lion	Tiger	Leopard	Jaguar	Puma
Fairy	Elf	Sprite	Mermaid	
Wood	Nymph			
Peacock	Kingfisher	Bird of Paradise	Flamingo	Bluebird
Orchid	Tiger Lilly	Sunflower	Fuchsia	Freesia

48

freedomprogramme@btinternet.com   www.freedomprogramme.co.uk

Printed by Amazon Italia Logistica S.r.l.
Torrazza Piemonte (TO), Italy

13631465R00030